A Sense of Science
Exploring Animal Life

Claire Llewellyn

SEA-TO-SEA
Mankato Collingwood London

This edition first published in 2009 by
Sea-to-Sea Publications
Distributed by Black Rabbit Books
P.O. Box 3263
Mankato, Minnesota 56002

Copyright text
© 2007, 2009 Claire Llewellyn
Copyright design and concept
© 2009 Sea-to-Sea Publications

Printed in China

All rights reserved.

Library of Congress
Cataloging-in-Publication Data:

Llewellyn, Claire.
  Exploring animal life / Claire Llewellyn.
    p. cm. -- (A sense of science)
  Includes index.
  Summary: "A simple exploration of animals that covers animal bodies, young, life cycles, and farm and pet animals, encouraging observation of the natural world. Includes activities"--Provided by publisher.
  ISBN 978-1-59771-126-5
  1. Animals--Miscellanea--Juvenile literature. I. Title.
  QL49L779 2009
  590--dc22
                                      2008007326

9 8 7 6 5 4 3 2

Published by arrangement with the
Watts Publishing Group Ltd, London.

Editor: Jeremy Smith
Art Director: Jonathan Hair
Design: Matthew Lilly
Cover and design concept:
Jonathan Hair

Photograph credits: Steve Shott, except:
Alamy: 7b, 15t, 17t, 25b.
Corbis: 4, 12, 24, 27.
istockphoto: 8, 9t, 10, 11b, 13, 16b,
17b, 18-19 all, 25t.

Contents

A world of animals	6
An animal's body	8
On the move	10
Mealtime	12
Baby animals	14
Growing up	16
Changing shape	18
Animal senses	20
On the farm	22
Animals at home	24
Caring for animals	26
Glossary	28
Activity: Make a creepy-crawly trap	29
Index	30

A world of animals

Animals live in the world around us.

Crabs live by the seashore.

All around
Which animals do you see where you live?

Rabbits live in fields.

We are animals too.

An animal's body

Animals' bodies are different from ours. A cat has fur all over its body.

Always wash your hands after touching an animal.

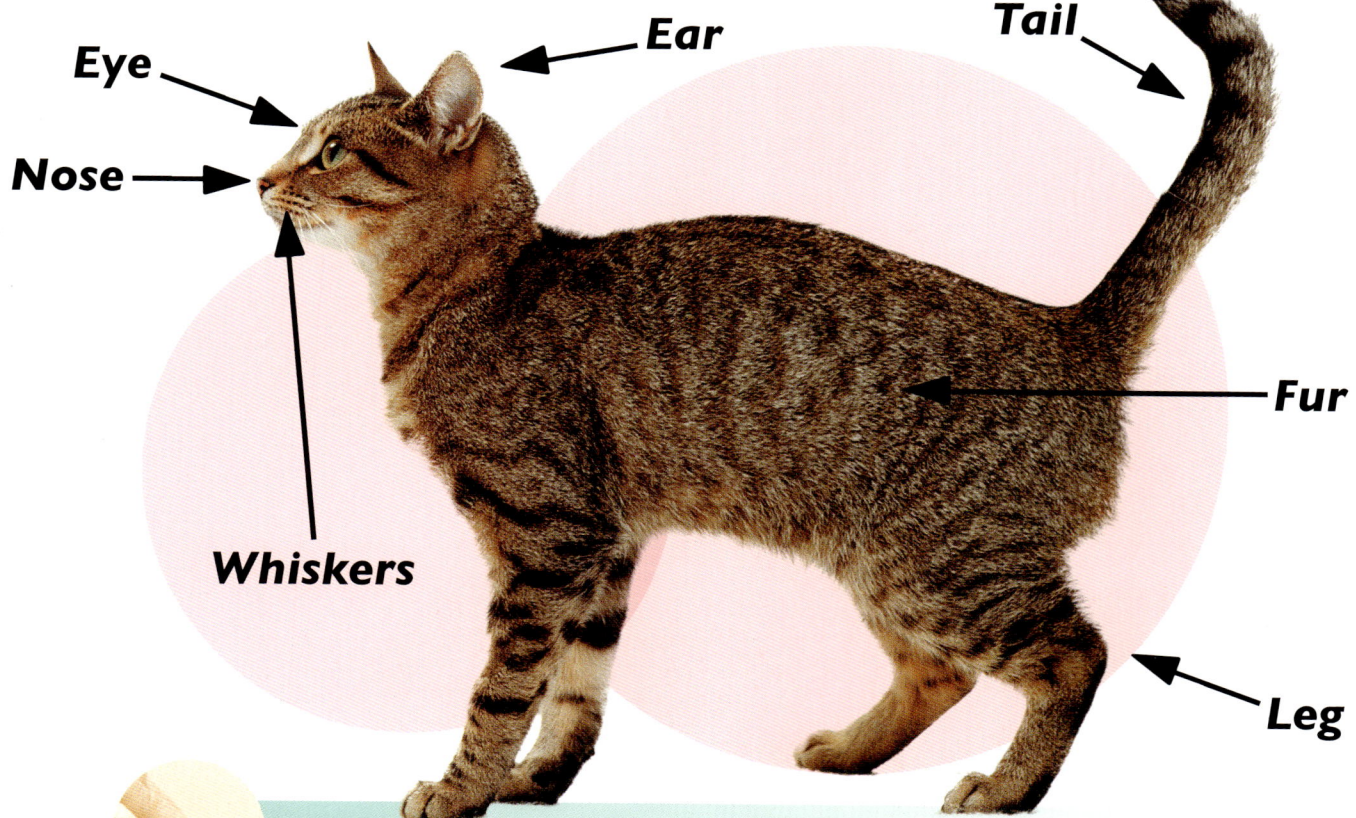

Eye
Nose
Ear
Tail
Fur
Whiskers
Leg

Touch and feel
Have you ever touched any animals? What did they feel like?

A bird has feathers and wings.

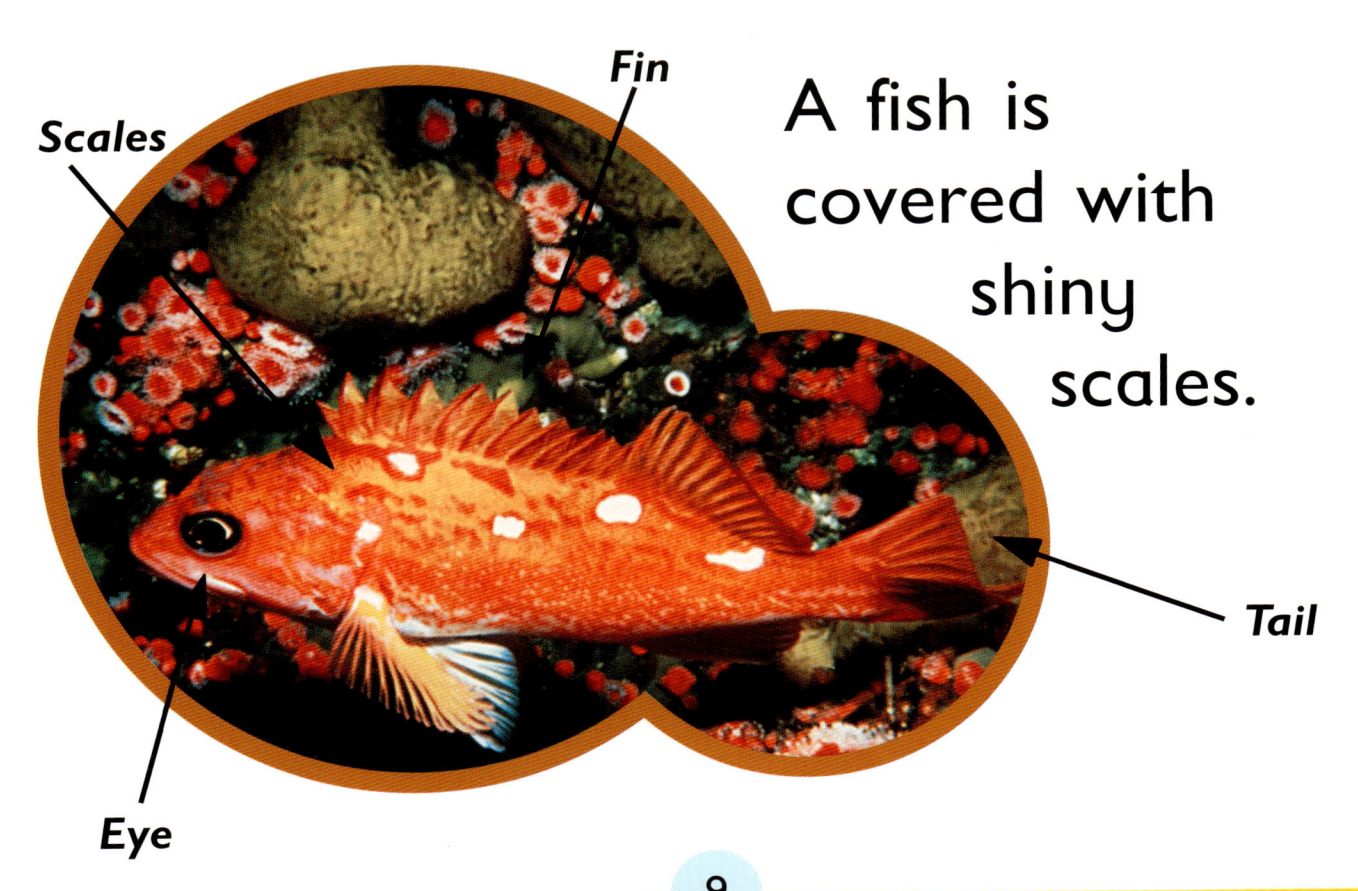

Feathers

Wing

Eye

Beak

Fin

Scales

A fish is covered with shiny scales.

Eye

Tail

On the move

Animals move in many different ways.

A butterfly flaps its wings to fly through the air.

Animal spotter
Look for some animals outside. How are they moving?

A horse runs on its four long legs.

A snake wriggles along the ground.

Mealtime

All animals need food and water to live.

Insect I-spy
Watch bees and butterflies on a warm, sunny day. Where do they feed?

A spider eats insects that it catches in its web.

A squirrel feeds on nuts.

This owl has caught a mouse.

Baby animals

All animals have young.

Baby talk
Look at the young animals in this picutres. What noises, if any, do they make?

This pig has had a piglet.

This mouse is looking after her young.

This caterpillar can look after itself. One day it will change into a butterfly.

Growing up

Baby animals change as they grow older.

Lambs grow bigger and stronger.

Young birds learn to fly.

Getting bigger
Children grow, too. How much taller than you are your mom and dad?

This kitten is learning to hunt.

Changing shape

Some animals change shape as they grow up.

A frog's eggs hatch into tiny tadpoles.

tadpole

egg

Look and learn
Look at the frog's eggs. How are they different from a bird's eggs?

 tadpole with back legs

As a tadpole gets bigger it grows legs.

 tadpole with front and back legs

The tadpole changes into a frog. It is an adult.

frog

Animal senses

Animals use their senses to find out about the world around them.

Sense it!
How do you use your eyes, ears, and nose to find out about the world around you?

A deer's ears help it hear danger.

A cat's eyes help it see at night.

A chicken can hear worms under the soil.

A fox can smell food from very far away!

On the farm

Some animals live on farms.

A farmer gives cattle food and shelter.

Good to eat
Look at the food inside your fridge. Did any of it came from farm animals?

Sheep give us wool, milk, and meat.

Chickens give us eggs and meat.

Animals at home

Pet animals live in our homes.

We feed and look after our pets.

Other animals live in our homes, too.

Some of them can be pests!

Creepy-crawly
Which small animals live in your home? Look around and see.

Caring for animals

Animals are living things.

We need to treat them with care.

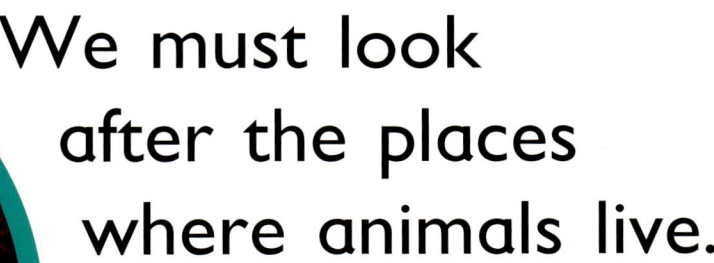

We must look after the places where animals live.

Winter watch

Put out food and water for the birds in winter. Which birds come to feed?

Never drop litter. It can harm wild animals.

Glossary

Claw
The sharp nail on the toe of an animal.

Fur
The hair that covers an animal's body.

Insects
A group of animals that are usually small and have six legs.

Litter
Garbage that we throw on the ground.

Pest
An animal that eats our plants or spoils our food.

Scales
The small, flat pieces that cover a fish's body.

Senses
The five different ways our body tells us about the world around us—by seeing, hearing, feeling, tasting, and smelling.

Shelter
A dry place to live.

Web
Sticky trap made by a spider.

Whiskers
Long fine hairs on the face of some animals.

Make a creepy-crawly trap

1. Find a glass jar. Put some leaves and soil in it and some scraps of apple or lettuce, or a tomato or cheese slice.

2. Sink the jar in the ground to soil level. Put a piece of wood on top of two stones to stop rain from getting into the jar.

3. Check your trap every day to see what you have caught. Try to find out the animals' names. Draw them and then let them go.

4. Put your trap in wet and dry places. Do you catch the same animals in each place?

Index

birds 9, 17, 18, 27
bodies 8-9, 28

caring for animals 22, 24, 26-27

ears 8, 20
eating 12-13
eyes 8, 9, 20, 21

farm animals 22-23
fish 9, 28
food 12-13, 21, 22-23, 27, 28
frog 18-19
fur 8, 28

growing up 16-19

insects 12, 28

moving 10-11

nose 8, 20

pets 24-25

scales 9, 28
senses 20-21, 28

young 14-15